Sip & Solve

LOGIC PUZZLES

MARK ZEGARELLI

Sterling Publishing Co., Inc.
New York

10 9 8 7 6 5 4 3

Published by Sterling Publishing Co., Inc.
387 Park Avenue South, New York, NY 10016

Distributed in Canada by Sterling Publishing
c/o Canadian Manda Group, 165 Dufferin Street
Toronto, Ontario, Canada M6K 3H6
Distributed in the United Kingdom by GMC Distribution Services
Castle Place, 166 High Street, Lewes, East Sussex, England BN7 1XU
Distributed in Australia by Capricorn Link (Australia) Pty. Ltd.
P.O. Box 704, Windsor, NSW 2756, Australia

Printed in China

Sterling ISBN-13: 978-1-4027-2989-8
ISBN-10: 1-4027-2989-8

For information about custom editions, special sales, premium and corporate purchases, please contact Sterling Special Sales Department at 800-805-5489 or specialsales@sterlingpub.com.

Contents

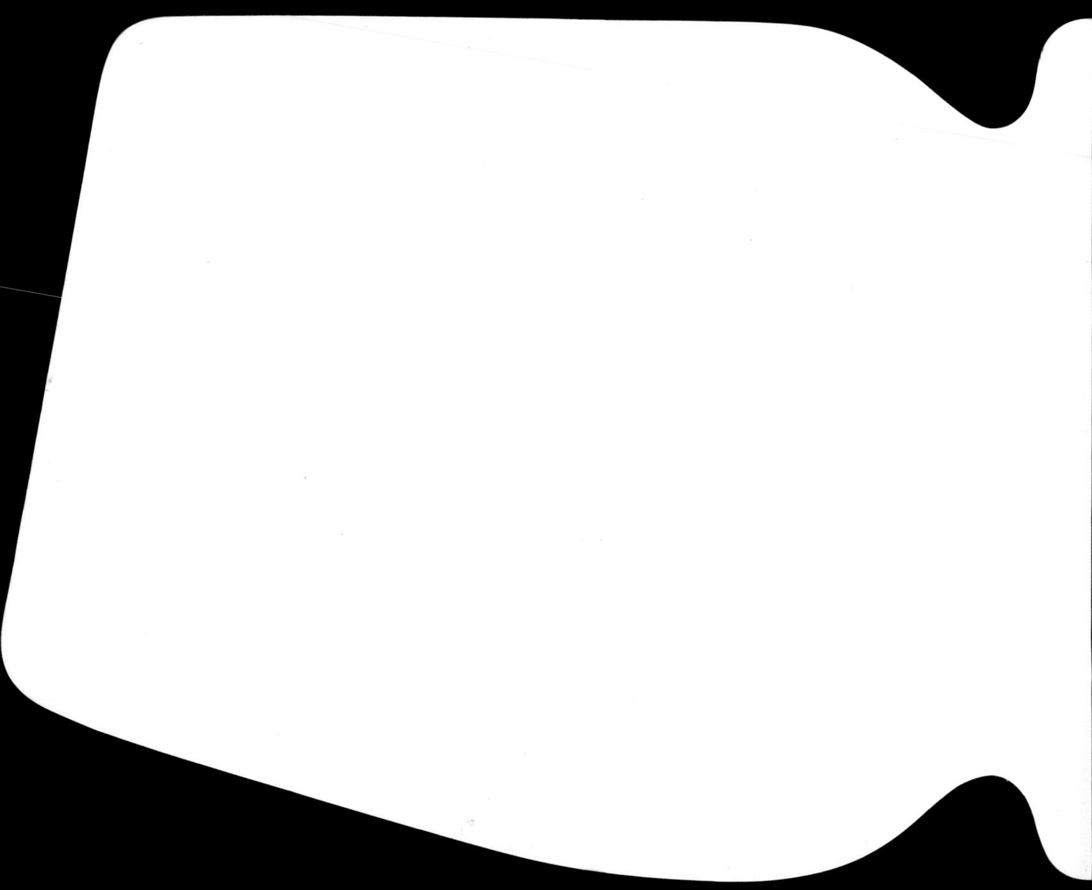

Introduction

What's a logic puzzle? A logic puzzle provides a short story plus some clues. Your job is to organize the information into the chart. That's it!

If you're new to logic puzzles, start with the first one in the book. When you figure it out, check to see if your answer is right. If it is, move on to the next.

The more you solve, the better you get. Solve the first 10 puzzles to give your brain a thorough stretch. If you get all the way to the end, consider yourself a first-rate logician.

Logic puzzles are a great way to pass the time, whether you're in a café, waiting for a train, or winding down before bed. Welcome, and good luck!

—Mark Zegarelli

HOW TO SOLVE LOGIC PUZZLES

Here are a few quick tips to get you started solving logic puzzles.

1. Anyone with a female-sounding name is a woman, and anyone with male-sounding name is a man. Surnames sound like surnames.

   Women: Alicia, Jessica, Karen, Christine, etc.

   Men: Luke, Frank, William, George, etc.
2. Husbands and wives are, respectively, male and female.
3. Solving a logic puzzle sort of like solving a jigsaw puzzle. Just try to fit all the information from the clues into the chart.
4. Sometimes, we start you off with a chart that is already partly filled-in. For example, in puzzle #1, "Zoo Story," the five years 2001 to 2005 are given in the chart. Now look at clue 1:

   "In 2001, Andy and Mavis visited either Longleat Safari Park or Whipsnade Wild Animal Park."

You can add both of these zoo names—Longleat and Whipsnade—directly into the chart in the box that's next to 2001. Remember, only one of them is correct, so you'll need to rule one of them out later on.

5. Every time you add to the chart, go back over the clues and look for the next piece that fits. In "Zoo Story," you will find that clue 2 is now helpful after you have added information from clue 1.
6. In harder puzzles, the charts start off empty, so you'll have to find clever ways to make the information fit. Keep trying and you'll soon get the hang of it. Practice makes perfect!

1 ZOO STORY

Andy and Mavis love animals and enjoy visiting zoos and safari parks that they have never seen before. In each of the last five years (2001 through 2005) they have visited a different zoo, three in their native England and two elsewhere. Can you discover the year in which they visited each zoo?

1. In 2001, Andy and Mavis visited either Longleat Safari Park or Whipsnade Wild Animal Park.
2. They made the trek to the U.S. to visit the famous San Diego Zoo three years before they visited Fota Wildlife Park in Cork, Ireland.
3. They didn't visit Chester Zoo or Longleat Safari Park in 2004.

Year	Zoo
2001	Longleat Safari Park LSP or WWAP
2002	San Diego Zoo
2003	Chester Zoo
2004	Whipsnade Wild Animal Park
2005	Fota WP; Cork Ireland

Answer, page 68

2 THREE-CAR GARAGE

Lydia buys and sells classic cars. She currently has three of them parked in her spacious garage, as shown at right. All three cars are different models (one is a Fairlane) and different colors (including pink). Use the clues to discover the position of all three cars in Lydia's garage and the color of each vehicle.

1. The Hudson is parked in space #1.
2. The Edsel is parked somewhere to the left of the blue car.
3. The green car isn't parked in space #2.

	#1 (left)	#2	#3 (right)
Car model	Hudson	Edsel	Fairlane
Color	Green	Pink	Blue

Answer, page 68

3 WINTER WUNDERKIND

Pilar moved from Ecuador to Nova Scotia when she was in third grade. Before that, she had never tried any winter sports, but in the next five years (from fourth grade to eighth grade), she joined five different teams in her new school and excelled at all five sports. Can you find out in which grade she joined each team?

1. In fourth grade, Pilar didn't join the figure skating team or the speed skating team.
2. In sixth grade, she didn't join the cross-country ski team.
3. Pilar joined the figure skating team either the year before or the year after she joined the downhill ski team.
4. She joined the cross-country ski team sometime after she joined the downhill ski team and sometime before she joined the ski jumping team.

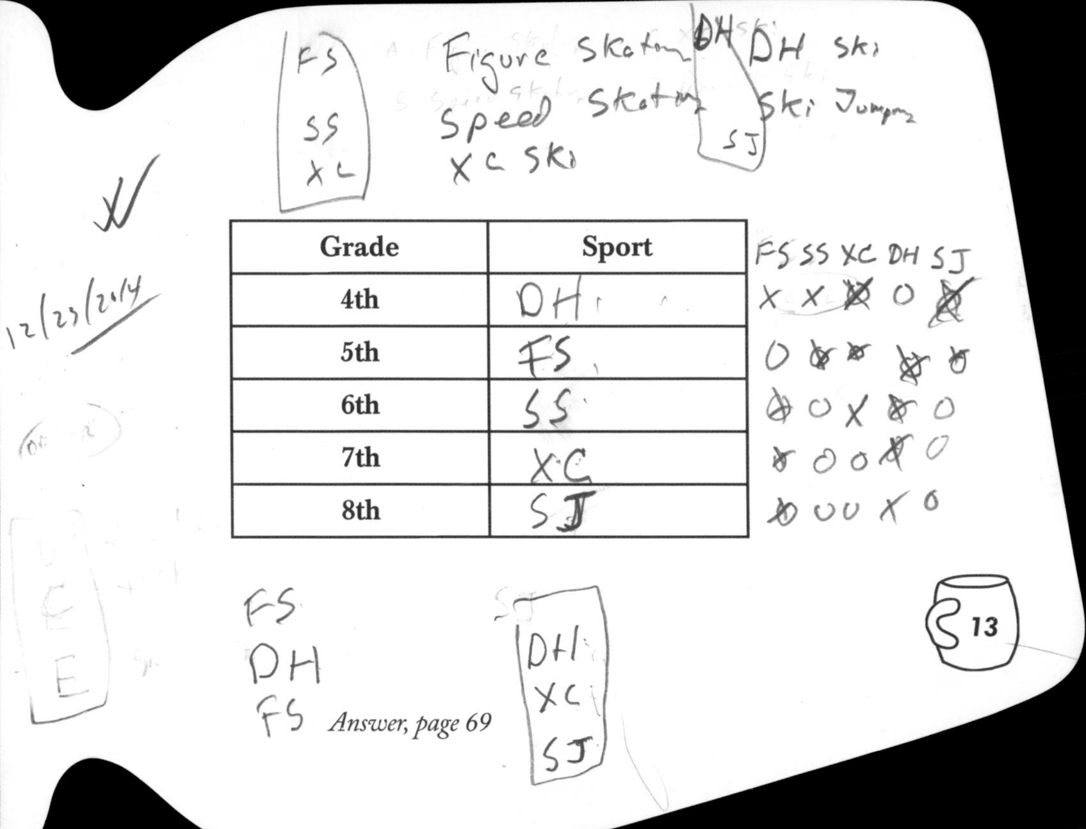

Grade	Sport
4th	
5th	
6th	
7th	
8th	

Answer, page 69

4 BANK SHOTS

As winter approached, four banks participated in a city-wide program immunization program. On four different days (Wednesday through Saturday), each bank provided a different volunteer physician a space to administer flu shots. Match up each day with the doctor who volunteered and the bank that provided space.

1. Union Reserve provided space on Wednesday.
2. Neither Commerce Savings nor the Regent's Bank provided space on Friday.
3. The Regent's Bank provided space for Dr. Whittaker, but not on Saturday.
4. Dr. Chan volunteered sometime before Dr. Krulikowski.
5. Neither First Federal nor Union Reserve provided space for Dr. Friedrich.

Day	Doctor	Bank
Wednesday		
Thursday		
Friday		
Saturday		

Answer, page 69

5 PIE-EATING CONTEST

At the annual Crust County Fair, the big event is the pie-eating contest. This year, out of a field of over 30 entrants, the first five people to finish their five-pound pies emerged with ribbons. Each winner ate a different type of pie (blueberry, cherry, coconut cream, apricot, or banana cream). Figure out the order in which these five people finished and the type of pie that each ate.

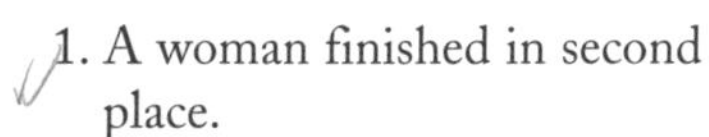

1. A woman finished in second place.
2. Calvin finished three places ahead of the person who ate a banana cream pie.
3. Norman, who ate either the apricot or the cherry pie, didn't finish third.
4. Mary finished her pie sometime before another person finished his or her blueberry pie.
5. Jasper didn't finish his pie just before the person who ate the apricot pie.
6. Ethel finished either just before or just after the person who ate a coconut cream pie.

Order	Person	Pie
1st		
2nd		
3rd		
4th		
5th		

Answer, page 70

6 WEEKLY CHORES

The four Taylor children do weekly chores around their house. When school is out during the summer, each child (including Patrick) is responsible for one indoor chore and one outdoor chore. Can you discover each child's two chores?

1. Erik washes either the interior or exterior windows, but not both.
2. Madeleine either trims the hedges or mows the lawn.
3. The child who cleans the bathroom doesn't also wash the exterior windows.
4. Emily either vacuums the downstairs or cleans the bathroom.
5. The child who does the dusting also weeds the garden.
6. The children who vacuum the downstairs and trim the hedges have different initials.
7. A boy washes the interior windows.

Erich windows inside outside
Madeleine trims hedges mows the lawn
cleans bathroom ∅ ext windows
Emily either vacuums or bathroom
dusting also weeds

Child	Inside chore	Outside chore
Patrick		
Erik		
Madeline		
Emily		

Answer, page 71

7 SOAK YOUR TROUBLES AWAY

Four couples in our neighborhood recently purchased hot tubs. Each bought a hot tub model named for a different sunny location and each model can accommodate a different number of people (four, five, six, or eight). Figure out how many people each model of hot tub can accommodate and which couple bought it.

1. The Palm Springs can hold exactly two more people than the South Beach.
2. Either the DeCraenes or the Wus bought the Key Largo.
3. The Santa Barbara can hold more people than the model that the Raftery s bought and fewer people than the model that the Gradys bought.
4. The Wus didn't buy the hot tub that holds five people.

Hot tubs

Number of people	Model	Last name
Four		
Five		
Six		
Eight		

Answer, page 71

8 HISTORIC WHARF STREET

Port James recently celebrated its tricentennial on its oldest thoroughfare, Wharf Street. The street fronts on the harbor and features four buildings, as shown at right, dating back to the early 17th century (one in 1714). Can you discover where each building is located and the year in which it was built?

1. The building that was completed in 1708 is somewhere west of the one that was built in 1711.
2. The Fish Market is somewhere west of the Armory.
3. The First Methodist Church was built in 1710.
4. The Old City Hall is building #3.
5. The Armory was built four years after building #4.

	#1 (west)	#2	#3	#4 (east)
Building				
Year				

Answer, page 72

9 IRISH FESTIVALS

Over mugs of green beer on St. Patrick's Day, five married couples at a local pub talked about the Irish festivals they had attended during the previous year. Can you discover who is married to whom (one woman's name is Angelica) and find out which festival each couple attended?

1. Kathryn isn't married to Bart or Philip.
2. Jacob didn't go to the Milwaukee Irish Fest.
3. Philip went to the Toledo Irish Festival.
4. Lenore went to the Irish Spring Festival in Ireland, West Virginia.
5. Rachel is married to either Jacob or Tyler.
6. Missy (who isn't married to Bart or Tyler) went to either the Colorado Irish Festival or the Milwaukee Irish Fest.
7. Either Bart or Nat went to the Philadelphia Ceili Group Festival.

Woman	Man	Festival

Answer, page 72

10 HAUNTED HOUSE

Every Halloween, Baker's Farm turns its barn into the biggest haunted house in the county. The attraction consists of a series of dark hallways connecting six main rooms, each housing a "live dead" actor playing a different scary character (including Lizzie Borden). Last year, the Bakers' six grandchildren (including Angela) walked through together. Each thought that a different room was the scariest. Discover the number of the room that scared each child and the character in each room.

1. The Spider Woman was in the room that the children entered just before the room that Tricia thought was the scariest.
2. The Werewolf was three rooms before the room that Stephen thought was the scariest.
3. Laureen thought that the third room was the scariest.
4. Vlad the Impaler awaited the children in the fourth room.
5. The room with Jack the Ripper was sometime after the room that Randall thought was the scariest.
6. The Snake Charmer was three rooms after the room that Bradley thought was the scariest.

Room	Child	Character
1st		
2nd		
3rd		
4th		
5th		
6th		

Answer, page 73

11 SPINNING YARNS

The old fashioned knitting circle is not completely out of fashion. Four women sat together yesterday, as shown at right, each knitting something different (including a pillow cover). Each told a different story (one spoke about how she quit smoking). Can you match up each woman's position in the circle, what she was knitting, and the story she told?

1. The woman who was knitting baby booties sat in seat #1.
2. Elise, who was knitting a sweater, told the story of her daughter's first piano recital.
3. Joannie wasn't knitting a scarf.
4. The woman who told the story of her childhood in Mississippi sat in seat #4.
5. Marion told the story of her cruise to Alaska.
6. Dolores sat in seat #3.

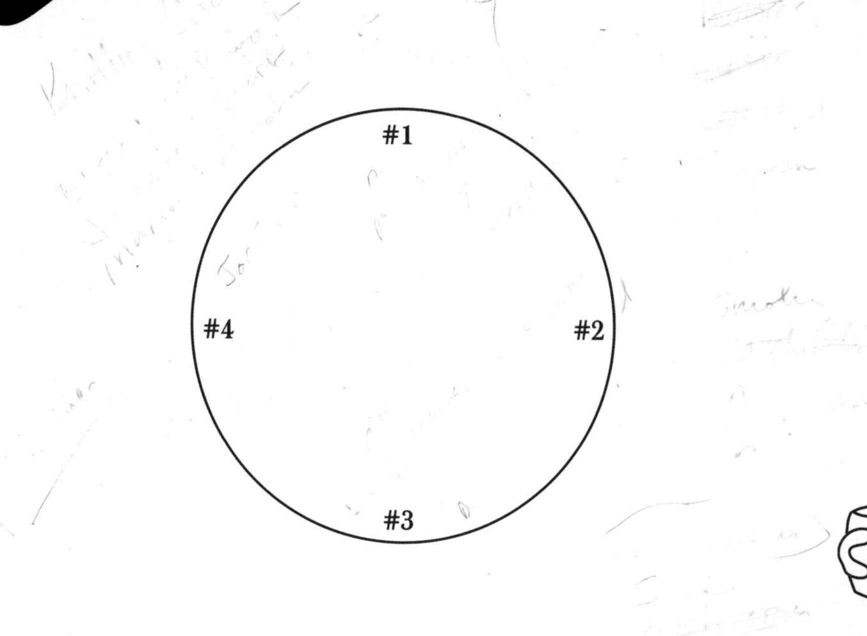

Answer, page 74

12 MEN WHO WEAR THE STAR

Even though he is a lieutenant-colonel in the U.S. Army, Evan Worth still has a lot to live up to. His four ancestors along his paternal line (father, grandfather, great grandfather, great-great-grandfather) were all generals, each retiring with a different number of stars (from one to four). See if you can figure out how each man was related to Evan and how many stars he achieved.

1. Martin was the grandson of the man who retired with one star.
2. Jacob wasn't Randolph's son.
3. Nathaniel retired with two more stars than Evan's great-grandfather.
4. Either Jacob or Martin retired as a three-star general.

Father
Grandfather
Great GF
GG GF

1
2
3
4

Martin
Jacob
Randolph
Nathaniel

Evan

Relationship	Man	Number of stars
Father	M N J R Nathaniel	4
Grandfather	M N J R Martin	3
Great Grandfather	J R Randolf	2
Great Great Grandfather	N J R Jacob	1

Evan Wirth

Answer, page 74

13 KEY WEST VACATION

Peter and Mark spent five days of their spring break in Key West. Each day (Tuesday through Saturday), they spent part of the day engaged in a different water activity (including sailing) and also rented a different mode of transportation. See if you can match up each day with its water activity and mode of transportation.

1. Peter and Mark went swimming the day after they went snorkeling and the day before they rented the dune buggy.
2. The day they went jetskiing (which wasn't Friday) wasn't the day that they rented the motorcycles.
3. They went scuba diving the day after they rented the scooters and the day before they rented the bicycles.
4. They rented the motorcycles and the electric car at least three days apart, in some order.

Day	Water activity	Transportation

Answer, page 75

14 WHOSE ROUND?

Four friends met for happy hour drinks. They sat at a round table, as shown at right, and over the course of the evening had four rounds of drinks. Each friend paid for a different round. Can you discover where each friend sat, his or her full name, and the order in which the four paid for drinks?

1. The first two people who paid for drinks sat across from each other.
2. Arnie paid for the round just after Millican.
3. Nieland, who didn't pay for the fourth round of drinks, paid for a round sometime after Beth did.
4. The person who sat in seat #2 and the person who bought the fourth round of drinks are of opposite sexes.
5. Clarice bought a round of drinks sometime after the person who sat in seat #1.
6. Kowalski and Lehmer sat across from each other.
7. Neither Dave nor Kowalski sat in seat #4.

#1

#4 #2

#3

Answer, page 77

15 JUST ADD SALT

When the doctor recommends cutting back on salt, certain foods lose their appeal. Five people (including Bertha and Howard) discovered this recently. Each found that he or she could no longer eat a different food without salt to bring out the flavor. Can you discover each person's full name and the food that he or she no longer eats?

1. Millie found that cantaloupe just isn't the same without that little sprinkle on top.
2. Four of the five people are: Judith, Albertson, Frame, and the person who gave up tomatoes.
3. Zachrisson and the person who gave up tomatoes are of opposite sexes.
4. The person who gave up hard-boiled eggs (who is a woman) isn't surnamed Lucelli.
5. Albertson and the person who gave up soft pretzels are of opposite sexes.
6. The person who gave up popcorn isn't surnamed Albertson or Lucelli.
7. Ernie (who isn't surnamed Frame or Meltzer) didn't give up soft pretzels or tomatoes.

First name	Last name	Food

Answer, page 78

16 HANDY WOMAN

Marie earns her living doing repairs for homeowners in her area. Over three days (Wednesday through Friday) she did a total of eight tasks for one client. Can you discover the order in which Marie did the eight tasks and the day on which she did each?

1. Marie's first tasks on the three days were, in some order: hanging the chandelier, installing the dimmer switches, and replacing floorboards.
2. She fixed screens at least one day before she installed weather stripping.
3. She did at least one more task on Thursday than she did the day she installed dimmer switches.
4. Marie caulked the shower sometime, but not immediately, before she painted the bathroom ceiling.
5. She did the same number of tasks on Wednesday as she did the day she hung the chandelier.
6. She repaired sheetrock sometime before she replaced the floorboards.
7. Marie did no more than five tasks on any single day.

Day	Order	Trash

Answer, page 79

17 A BEE IN SPELLING

Five children from Richard Widmark Junior High School (including Bonnie) went to the State Spelling Bee Championship. Although none won the tournament, they all scored among the top thirty (4th, 9th, 15th, 20th, and 26th). Each misspelled a different word. Can you figure out each child's ranking in the tournament and the word that he or she misspelled?

1. A boy misspelled "ecchymosis."
2. Brenda ranked exactly five places behind the child who misspelled "hauberk."
3. Byron didn't rank exactly six places ahead of the child who misspelled "vendaval."
4. The five children are: Benjamin, Brenda, the children who misspelled "rascette" and "vendaval," and the child who ranked 20th.
5. Brad ranked either six places ahead of or six places behind the child who misspelled "klendusity."

Rank	Child	Word

Answer, page 81

18 NINE DAYS, NINE CITIES

Roscoe is regional manager for a chain of successful toy stores in New York, New Jersey, and Pennsylvania. During the Christmas season last year he worked ten consecutive days, each day at a different location: four in New York (Albany, Rochester, Rye, and Syracuse), three in New Jersey (Newark, Teaneck, and Trenton), and two in Pennsylvania (Bethlehem and Scranton). Can you discover the order in which he was in these locations?

1. Each day, Roscoe found himself in a different state from the previous day.
2. He visited all four cities in New York sometime after visiting Bethlehem and sometime before visiting Trenton.
3. He didn't visit Newark three days after he visited Rochester.
4. Four cities that he visited in order, but not necessarily consecutively, are: Teaneck, Rye, Albany, and Scranton.
5. Roscoe never crossed the state line between New Jersey and Pennsylvania.

Day	City
1st	
2nd	
3rd	
4th	
5th	
6th	
7th	
8th	
9th	

Answer, page 82

19 GOLDEN EGGS

Every Easter, our local Chamber of Commerce hosts an egg hunt in Memorial Park. Among the many eggs filled with chocolate and small prizes, five golden eggs are hidden containing $100 gift certificates to local shops (Marina's Jewelry, Dale's Music Shop, Ristorante Via Venezia, Have a Ball Sporting Goods, Captain Video). A different child (including Paul) found each egg in a different place (including in a fountain). Can you discover where each child found a golden egg and the gift certificate it contained?

1. The boy who won a gift certificate for Dale's Music Shop didn't find in the birdfeeder.
2. The egg hidden inside a cannon didn't contain a gift certificate for Have-a-Ball Sporting Goods.
3. Jasmine won a gift certificate for either Captain Video Games or Marina's Jewelry.
4. Ellen found an egg either inside a cannon or under a picnic table.
5. The child who found an egg beneath a trash can (who isn't Keith) didn't win a gift certificate to Ristorante Via Venezia.

6. The five children are: Regina, the children who found eggs in a birdfeeder and under a picnic table, and the children who won gift certificates for Captain Video Games and Have-a-Ball Sporting Goods.

Child	Location	Gift certificate

Answer, page 83

20 HAZARDOUS HOBBIES

Four good friends (including Beverly and Herman), all known as daredevils, used to enjoy different activities until he or she had an accident that resulted in injury (including a broken wrist). From then on, he or she took developed a more sedentary interest. Discover each person hazardous hobby, the injury he or she sustained, and his or her new interest.

1. The woman who took up collecting model trains didn't displace a vertebra.
2. A man used to do parasailing.
3. The bungee jumper dislocated his or her shoulder.
4. Neither Margie (who took up birdwatching) nor Stuart (who didn't take up butterfly collecting) is the former skydiver.
5. The hang gliding accident didn't result in a displaced vertebra.
6. The person who now juggles beanbags (who didn't fracture his or her tibia) has never done bungee jumping or parasailing.

Person	Hazardous hobby	Injury	New hobby

Answer, page 84

21 ROYALTY CHECKS

Peter is a photojournalist and author of a successful series of books on seven current European monarchs (including Albert II of Belgium and Margrethe II of Denmark). Last year, he received one royalty check for each book, each in a different month. Can you discover the month in which he received a check for each book?

1. Peter received a check for the book on Prince Rainier III of Monaco in either February or November.
2. He received the check for the book on King Juan Carlos of Spain during a month whose initial is J.
3. One of the first two royalty checks that Peter received was for the book on King Carl XVI Gustav of Sweden.
4. He received the check for the book on King Harald V of Norway in either July or September.
5. The only two checks Peter received in consecutive months were for the books on Queen Beatrix of the Netherlands and another ruler, in some order.

6. He received checks for the two female rulers no more than four months apart.

Month	Book (monarch)

Answer, page 85

22 AMY'S ADVICE

Amy writes the advice column for a small weekly newspaper. At the end of her column, she provides short responses to advice seekers who have requested that she not publish their letters. This week, she included five such responses. Can you figure out the order in which she addressed these five people and the advice she gave?

1. Amy's first response was to either Bewildered Boss or Perplexed Patron.
2. Her response to Furious Father was "I would have gone ballistic."
3. She responded to Curious Cousin sometime before her response "Lighten up, dear."
4. Amy's response to Curious Cousin wasn't just before her response to Distraught Daughter; her advice to one of these two people was "Learn to speak Spanish."
5. Her response to Bewildered Boss was either just before or just after her response "Not on your life."
6. Her second or third response was "You're only fooling yourself."
7. Amy's fifth response was either "Lighten up, dear" or "Not on your life."

Order	Person	Advice

Answer, page 86

23 SILENT FILM FESTIVAL

The Lumiere Theater held its annual Silent Film festival. From Monday through Saturday, two silent film stars—one female and the other male (including Charlie Chaplin)—were featured every day. For each day of the film festival, can you discover the featured female and male stars?

1. Mary Astor and William Desmond Taylor were featured on the same day.
2. Betty Blythe was featured either the day before or the day after Buster Keaton.
3. Theda Bara was featured four days before Rudolph Valentino.
4. On Friday, the featured male star was either Buster Keaton or Douglas Fairbanks.
5. Louise Brooks was featured the day before Mary Pickford.
6. Clara Bow was featured two days before Fatty Arbuckle.

Day	Female star	Male star
Monday		
Tuesday		
Wednesday		
Thursday		
Friday		
Saturday		

Answer, page 87

24 GREEN ACRES, THE MUSICAL

This season's off-Broadway hit is a brand new musical based on the TV comedy *Green Acres*. The five songs from the first act of the show (including "One Tiny Seed") are sung by different combinations of the five main characters. Can you figure out which characters participate in each song?

1. Each song is sung by a different number of people (from one to five).
2. Oliver, Lisa, and one nosy intruder sing the humorous "Just Us Two."
3. Mr. Kimball's only two songs are "Civil Service Blues" and "Down on the Farm."
4. Lisa and Eb don't sing the same number of songs.
5. Oliver sings a solo.
6. Eb doesn't sing both "Civil Service Blues" and "Just Us Two."
7. Lisa and Mr. Haney sing just two songs together, including "Hotcakes in Hooterville."

Song	Singer(s)

Answer, page 88

25 HANGOVER CURES

Terry had a bit too much fun on Saturday night. On Sunday morning, he complained of hangover to five friends (including Therese). Each recommended a different over-the-counter medicine with a different food item. See if you can figure out which medicine and food item each recommended.

1. The five friends are: Barbara, Calvin, the person who recommended aspirin, and the people who recommended jelly beans and Ritz crackers.
2. The person who recommended Excedrin (who isn't Larry) didn't recommend cherries.
3. The friend who recommended ginger snaps also recommended either aspirin or Tylenol.
4. The people who recommended Excedrin and ibuprofen are of the same sex.
5. The five friends are: Jenny, the people who recommended Aleve and Excedrin, and the people who recommended jelly beans and olives.

Person	Medicine	Food

Answer, page 89

26 SCRABBLE BINGOS

Benny and three of his friends play Scrabble. In their last game, each person scored one "bingo" by placing all seven of his or her letters in one turn to spell a different word (including "tremors"). Can you discover the order in which these people scored the bingos, each person's full name (one surname is Pantella), and the word each spelled?

1. The four people are: Adrienne, Brown, the person who placed the word "beckoned," and the person who placed the first bingo.
2. The four people are: Prudence, Ackerman, the person who placed the word "painting," and the person who placed the second bingo.
3. The four people are: Tami, Torricelli, the person who placed the word "alchemy," and the person who placed the third bingo.
4. One person's first name, last name, and bingo all have the same initial; the other three people's first name, last name, and bingo all have different initials.

Order	First name	Last name	Word

Answer, page 90

27 UNCONVENTIONAL CONVENTIONERS

At a recent *Star Trek* convention, Trey and four other fans engaged in a heated discussion about which of the five series was the best. Each was dressed as a different type of alien and each had a different reason for preferring one series over the others (one liked the episode plots). Discover each person's costume, his or her favorite series, and the reason in each case.

1. The person dressed as a Romulan likes *Voyager* best.
2. Either Anton or Marie was dressed as a Borg.
3. Four of the five people are: Marie, the person dressed as a Klingon, the person who likes *Deep Space Nine* best, and the person who likes a series for the quality of its acting.
4. Sue (who wasn't dressed as a Ferengi or a Romulan) didn't stress characters or special effects.
5. The person who likes a series for its characters was dressed as either a Klingon or a Vulcan.

6. Jaime (whose favorite show is *The Next Generation*) wasn't dressed as a Klingon.
7. Anton likes a series either for its special effects or for overall storyline.
8. The person dressed as a Ferengi prefers either *Star Trek* or *Deep Space Nine*.
9. One person prefers *Enterprise* for its special effects.

Person	Costume	Series	Reason

Answer, page 91

28 SHOW ME THE MUNI

Last night, five young men in San Francisco (including Leroy and Micah) took Muni trains to visit their girlfriends (including Joanie and Nona). Each of them took a different line (including the N). Each young man, his girlfriend, and the line that he took have three different initials. See if you can match up each man with his girlfriend and the line that he took to visit her.

1. Only the K, L, and M lines go to West Portal.
2. Only the J, K, and M lines go to Balboa Park.
3. Kyle's girlfriend is Monica.
4. Linda lives in West Portal.
5. Noah took the L line.
6. Jason's girlfriend lives in Balboa Park.
7. Katy lives in the same neighborhood as the woman whose boyfriend took the M.

Man	Girlfriend	Line

Answer, page 92

29 THE MEDIUM AND THE MESSAGE

As an independent project for her master's degree in psychology, Joan did an informal study of psychic phenomena. She called four different psychic hotlines, in each case speaking to a different medium. Each attributed Joan with a different career, marital status (including single), domicile (including a trailer), and eye color. Each medium was right only once. Figure out which medium attributed each of these four attributes to Joan, and which four attributes accurately describe her.

1. Selenia was half right when she thought that Joan was a married nurse.
2. One medium thought she was a brown-eyed divorcée who lived in an apartment.
3. Either Isis or Zayne thought Joan was a blue-eyed teacher.
4. The four mediums are: Isis, the person who thought that Joan is a widow, the one who thought that she lives in a house, and the one who knew her correct eye color.
5. Konstantin was right either about Joan's eye color or living situation.

6. One medium was completely wrong in thinking that Joan is a green-eyed accountant.
7. Joan is either a shop owner, has hazel eyes (as one medium thought), or both.
8. She is either divorced or lives in a condominium, or both.

Medium	Career	Marital status	Domicile	Eye color

Answer, page 93

30 ROAD SIGNS

Five friends are all into astrology, so much so that each drives a car named for a different zodiac sign (one drives a Libra). By a curious coincidence, in each case one of the other four people was born under each of these signs. Can you discover each person's full name, the car he or she drives, and his or her zodiac sign? Note: Daisy and Lillian are women; Jonathan is a man; Pat and Robin could be of either sex.

1. Pat's zodiac sign is the same as Reynaud's car.
2. Mr. Zeff drives either an Aries or a Scorpio.
3. Jonathan and Pat are, in some order, the person who drives a Taurus and the person born under this sign.
4. Daisy's car is the same as Mr. Waitman's zodiac sign, and her zodiac sign is the same as Ms. Chandler's car.
5. The people who drive the Aries and the Virgo are of opposite sexes.
6. The person born under Scorpio (who is either Lillian or Robin) is surnamed either Taylor or Zeff.
7. Neither Daisy nor Robin drives an Aries.

Mr./Mrs.	First name	Last name	Car	Sign

Answer, page 94

1 ZOO STORY

In 2001, Andy and Mavis visited either Longleat Safari Park or Whipsnade Wild Animal Park in 2001 (1). They didn't visit the San Diego Zoo in 2003, 2004, or 2005 (2), so they visited it in 2002 and visited the Fota Wildlife Park in 2005 (2). They didn't visit Chester or Longleat in 2004 (3), so they visited Whipsnade in 2004. They visited Longleat in 2001 (1). By elimination, they visited Chester in 2003.

2001	Longleat Safari Park
2002	San Diego Zoo
2003	Chester Zoo
2004	Whipsnade Wild Animal Park
2005	Fota Wildlife Park

2 THREE-CAR GARAGE

The Hudson is parked in space #1 (1). The Edsel isn't parked in space #3 (2), so it's parked in space #2. By elimination, the Fairlane is parked in space #3, and it is blue (2). The green car isn't parked in space #2 (3), so it's in space #1; therefore, it's the Hudson. By elimination, the Edsel is pink.

#1	Hudson	green
#2	Edsel	pink
#3	Fairlane	blue

3 WINTER WUNDERKIND

In fourth grade, Pilar didn't join figure skating team or the speed skating team (1), or the cross-country ski or ski-jumping team (4), so she joined the downhill ski team. She joined the figure skating team in fifth grade (3). She didn't join the cross-country ski team in sixth grade (2) or eighth grade (4), so she joined it in seventh grade. She joined the ski-jumping team in eight grade (4). By elimination, she joined the speed skating team in sixth grade.

4th	downhill ski
5th	figure skating
6th	speed skating
7th	cross-country
8th	ski jumping

4 BANK SHOTS

Union Reserve provided space on Wednesday (1). Neither Commerce Savings nor the Regent's Bank provided space on Friday (2), so First Federal did. The bank that provided space on Saturday isn't the Regent's bank (3), so it is Commerce Savings. By elimination, the Regents Bank provided space on Thursday for Dr. Whittaker (3). Neither First Federal nor Union Reserve provided space for Dr. Friedrich (4), so Commerce Savings did. Dr. Chan volunteered on Wednesday and Dr. Krulikowski on Thursday (4).

Wed.	Dr. Chan	Union Reserve
Thu.	Dr. Whittaker	Regent's Bank
Fri.	Dr. Krulikowski	First Federal
Sat.	Dr. Friedrich	Commerce Savings

5 PIE-EATING CONTEST

A woman finished in second place (1), so this was either Ethel or Mary. Calvin didn't finish third, fourth, or fifth (2), so he finished first and the person who ate a banana cream pie finished fourth. Norman ate either the apricot or the cherry pie and didn't finish third (3), so he finished fifth. Mary finished second and the person who ate blueberry pie finished third (4). Ethel finished third and Mary ate the coconut cream pie (6). By elimination, Jasper finished fourth. Norman finished just after him (see above), so he didn't eat the apricot pie (5), so he ate the cherry pie. By elimination, Calvin ate the apricot pie.

First	Calvin	apricot
Second	Mary	coconut cream
Third	Ethel	blueberry
Fourth	Jasper	banana cream
Fifth	Norman	cherry

6 WEEKLY CHORES

Madeleine either trims the hedges or mows the lawn (2). Emily either vacuums the downstairs or cleans the bathroom (4). The child who does the dusting also weeds the garden (5). This isn't Erik (1), so this is Patrick. Erik washes the interior windows (7). He doesn't wash the exterior windows (1), so Emily does. She doesn't clean the bathroom (3), so Madeleine does. By elimination, Emily vacuums. Erik doesn't trim the hedges (6), so Madeleine does. By elimination, Erik mows the lawn.

Emily	vacuums	ext. windows
Erik	int. windows	lawn
Madeleine	bathroom	hedges
Patrick	dusting	weeding

7 SOAK YOUR TROUBLES AWAY

The Palm Springs can hold exactly two more people than the South Beach (1), so one of these models can hold exactly six people. The Santa Barbara doesn't accommodate either four or eight people (3), so it holds five people. The Rafterys bought the hot tub that holds four people (3). Either the DeCraenes or the Wus bought the Key Largo (2), so this model holds eight people. The Palm Springs holds six people and the South Beach holds four (1). The Gradys didn't buy the Santa Barbara (3), so they bought the Palm Springs. The Wus didn't buy the Santa Monica (4), so they bought the Key Largo. By elimination, the DeCraenes bought the Santa Barbara.

Four	South Beach	Raftery
Five	Santa Barbara	DeCraene
Six	Palm Springs	Grady
Eight	Key Largo	Wu

8 HISTORIC WHARF STREET

The Old City Hall is building #3 (4). The Armory isn't #4 (5), so it's #2 and the Fish Market is #1 (2). By elimination, the First Methodist Church is #4. This was built in 1710 (3). The Armory was built in 1714 (5). The Fish Market was built in 1708 and the Old City Hall was built in 1711.

#1	Fish Market	1708
#2	Armory	1714
#3	Old City Hall	1711
#4	First Methodist	1710

9 IRISH FESTIVALS

Philip went to the Toledo Irish Festival (3). Lenore went to the Irish Spring Festival (4). Rachel is married to either Jacob or Tyler (5). Missy went to either the Colorado Irish Festival or the Milwaukee Irish Fest (6). Either Bart or Nat went to the Philadelphia Ceili Group Festival (7). This accounts for the five couples. Kathryn isn't married to Philip (1), so she attended the Philadelphia Ceili Group Festival. She isn't married to Bart (1), so she's married to Nat. By elimination, Angelica is married to Philip. Missy isn't married to Bart or Tyler (6), so she's married to Jacob. Rachel is married to Tyler (5). By elimination, Lenore is married to Bart. Jacob and Missy didn't go to the Milwaukee Irish Fest (2), so they went to the Colorado Irish Festival. By elimination, Rachel and Tyler went to the Milwaukee Irish Fest.

Angelica	Philip	Toledo Irish Festival
Kathryn	Nat	Phila. Ceili Gp. Festival
Lenore	Bart	Irish Spring Festival
Missy	Jacob	Colorado Irish Festival
Rachel	Tyler	Milwaukee Irish Fest

10 HAUNTED HOUSE

Laureen thought the third room was the scariest (3). Vlad the Impaler was in the fourth room (4). The Snake Charmer was in the fifth room and Bradley thought the second room was scariest (6). The Spider Woman was in the third room and Tricia thought the fourth room was the scariest (1). The Werewolf was in the second room and Stephen thought the fifth room was scariest (2). The sixth room had Jack the Ripper and Randall thought the first room was scariest (5). By elimination, Angela thought the sixth room was scariest and Lizzie Borden was in the first room.

First	Randall	Lizzie Borden
Second	Bradley	Werewolf
Third	Laureen	Spider Woman
Fourth	Tricia	Vlad the Impaler
Fifth	Stephen	Snake Charmer
Sixth	Angela	Jack the Ripper

11 SPINNING YARNS

The woman who was knitting baby booties sat in seat #1 (1). The woman who told the story of her childhood in Mississippi sat in #4 (4). Dolores sat in seat #3 (6). Elise, who was knitting a sweater, told the story of her daughter's first piano recital (2), so she sat in #1. Marion told the story of her cruise to Alaska (5) and so must be in seat #1. By elimination, Joannie sat in #4 and Dolores talked about how she quit smoking. Joannie wasn't knitting a scarf (3), so Dolores was. By elimination, Joannie was knitting a pillow cover.

#1	Marion	baby booties	Alaska
#2	Elise	sweater	piano recital
#3	Dolores	scarf	quit smoking
#4	Joannie	pillow cover	Mississippi

12 MEN WHO WEAR THE STAR

Either Jacob or Martin retired as a three-star general (4). Nathaniel didn't retire with one or two stars (3), so he retired with four stars and Evan's great-grandfather retired with two (3). The man who retired with one star wasn't Evan's father or grandfather (1), so he was Evan's great-great-grandfather. Martin was this man's grandson (1), so he was Evan's grandfather. Thus, he didn't retire with one, two, or four stars (see above), so he retired with three stars. By elimination, Evan's father retired with four stars, so he was Nathaniel (see above). If Randolph had been Evan's great-great-grandfather, then by elimination Jacob would have been Evan's great-grandfather. In that case, however, Jacob would have been Randolph's son, which is impossible (2). Thus, Randolph was Evan's great-grandfather. By elimination, Jacob was Evan's great-great-grandfather.

Father	Nathaniel	four
Grandfather	Martin	three
Great-grandfather	Randolph	two
Great-great-grandfather	Jacob	one

13 KEY WEST VACATION

Clue 1 mentions three consecutive days of the trip and so does clue 3. Peter and Mark didn't go scuba diving more than one day before they went snorkeling, because then they would have rented scooters more than four days before they rented the dune buggy (1 & 3), which is impossible (intro) If they had gone scuba diving the day before they went snorkeling, then they would have rented scooters on Tuesday, bicycles on Thursday, and the dune buggy on Saturday (1 & 3). In this case, however, they would have rented motorcycles and the electric car on Wednesday and Friday, in some order, which is impossible (4). Thus, Peter and Mark went scuba diving sometime after they went snorkeling. This could only have been two days afterward (1 & 3). Thus, putting together the information in clues 1 and

3, we can conclude that four consecutive days of the trip were: the day they went snorkeling, the day they went swimming and rented scooters, the day they went scuba diving and rented the dune buggy, and the day they rented bicycles. They rented motorcycles and the electric car at least three days apart (4), so they rented these on Tuesday and Saturday, in some order. Thus, they went snorkeling on Tuesday, swimming on Wednesday, scuba diving on Thursday, and rented bicycles on Friday. They didn't go jetskiing on Friday (2), so they went sailing on Friday. By elimination, they went jetskiing on Saturday. They didn't rent the motorcycles on Saturday (2), so they rented the electric car on Saturday. By elimination, they rented motorcycles on Tuesday.

Tuesday	snorkeling	motorcycles
Wednesday	swimming	scooters
Thursday	scuba diving	dune buggy
Friday	sailing	bicycles
Saturday	jetskiing	electric car

14 WHOSE ROUND?

The first two people who paid for drinks sat across from each other (1), so, by elimination, the third and fourth people also sat across from each other. Kowalski and Lehmer sat across from each other (6), so, similarly, Millican and Nieland sat across from each other. Millican didn't pay for the fourth round (2) and neither did Nieland (3), so they paid for the first and second rounds, in some order (see above). Nieland didn't pay for the first round (3), so Millican did, and Nieland paid for the second round. Thus, Arnie is Nieland (2) and Beth is Millican (3). Dave isn't Kowalski (7), so Dave is Lehmer. By elimination, Clarice is Kowalski. She didn't sit in seat #4 (7) or seat #1 (8). Dave Lehmer sat across from her (see above), and he didn't sit in seat # 4 (7), so Clarice didn't sit in seat #2. Thus, Clarice sat in seat #3. Dave Lehmer sat across from her in seat #1 (see above), so he bought the third round and Clarice bought the fourth (5). A man sat in #2 (4), so he's Arnie. By elimination, Beth sat in #4.

#1	Dave Lehmer	third round
#2	Arnie Nieland	second round
#3	Clarice Kowalski	fourth round
#4	Beth Millican	first round

15 JUST ADD SALT

Millie no longer eats cantaloupe (1). Ernie didn't give up hardboiled eggs (4), or soft pretzels or tomatoes (7), so he gave up popcorn. He isn't surnamed Albertson or Lucelli (6), or Frame or Meltzer (7), so he's surnamed Zachrisson. A woman gave up tomatoes (3), but she isn't Judith (2) or Millie (1), so she's Bertha. Judith gave up hardboiled eggs (4). By elimination, Howard gave up soft pretzels. Albertson is a woman (5), but she isn't Judith or Bertha (2), so she's Millie. Frame isn't Judith or Bertha (2), so he's Howard. We know that Judith gave up hardboiled eggs, so she isn't Lucelli (4), so she's Meltzer. By elimination, Bertha is Lucelli.

Bertha Lucelli	tomatoes
Ernie Zachrisson	popcorn
Howard Frame	soft pretzels
Judith Meltzer	hardboiled eggs
Millie Albertson	cantaloupe

16 HANDY WOMAN

If Marie had done only one task on Wednesday, then she would have also done only one on another day (5), and six on the remaining day (intro), which is impossible (7). If she had done exactly four tasks on Wednesday, then she would have also done four on another day (5) and none on the remaining day (intro), which is impossible (1). If Marie had done exactly five tasks on Wednesday, then she would have done five on another day (5), which is impossible (intro). Marie did no more than five tasks each day (7), so she did either two or three tasks on Wednesday. If Marie had done three tasks on Wednesday, she would have done three on another day (5) and two on the remaining day (intro). Thus, she would have done three tasks on Thursday (3) and two on Friday, so she would have installed the dimmer switches on Friday (3) and hung the chandelier on Thursday (5). In this case, however, her first job on Wednesday would have been to replace the floorboards (1), which is impossible (6). Therefore, Marie did two tasks on Wednesday. She did two on another day (5) and four on the remaining day (intro). Thus, she did four tasks on Thursday (3) and, by elimination, two on Friday. She hung the chandelier on Friday (5), and this was her first task that day (1). She didn't install the dimmer switches on Friday (1) or Thursday (3), so she did this task on Wednesday, and it was her first task that day (1). Her first task on Thursday was replacing the floorboards (1). Her second task on Wednesday was to repair sheetrock (6). Her second task on Friday was to install weather stripping (2). On Thursday, her second task was caulking the shower and her fourth was painting the bathroom ceiling (4). By elimination, her third task on Thursday was to fix the screens.

Wed.	first	installed dimmer switches
	second	repaired sheetrock
Thu.	first	replaced floorboards
	second	caulked shower
	third	fixed screens
	fourth	painted bathroom ceiling
Fri.	first	hung chandelier
	second	installed weather stripping

17 A BEE IN SPELLING

The five children are: Benjamin, Brenda, the children who misspelled "rascette" and "vendaval," and the child who ranked 20th (4). Brenda ranked ninth (2). The child who misspelled "hauberk" ranked fourth (2), so he's Benjamin. A boy misspelled "ecchymosis" (1), so he ranked 20th. By elimination, Brenda misspelled "klendusity." Brad ranked 15th (5). By elimination, the boy who ranked 20th (see above) is Byron. Also by elimination, Bonnie ranked 26th. She didn't misspell "vendaval" (3), so she misspelled "rascette." By elimination, Brad misspelled "vendaval."

4th	Benjamin	"hauberk"
9th	Brenda	"klendusity"
15th	Brad	"vendaval"
20th	Byron	"ecchymosis"
26th	Bonnie	"rascette"

18 NINE DAYS, NINE CITIES

Roscoe crossed a state line every night (1), but never crossed the state line between New Jersey and Pennsylvania (6), so he was in New York on the second, fourth, sixth, and eighth days. He visited Bethlehem on the first day and Trenton on the ninth (2). He visited Rye fourth and Albany sixth (4). He visited Teaneck third and Scranton seventh (4). By elimination, he visited Newark fifth. On the second day, he didn't visit Rochester (3), so he visited Syracuse. By elimination, he visited Rochester on the eighth day.

1st	Bethlehem, PA
2nd	Syracuse, NY
3rd	Teaneck, NJ
4th	Rye, NY
5th	Newark, NJ
6th	Albany, NY
7th	Scranton, PA
8th	Rochester, NY
9th	Trenton, NJ

19 GOLDEN EGGS

The five children are: Regina, the children who found eggs in a birdfeeder and under a picnic table, and the children who won gift certificates for Captain Video and Have-a-Ball Sporting Goods (6). The boy who won a gift certificate for Dale's Music Shop didn't find in the birdfeeder (1), so he found it under a picnic table. Ellen can't be this boy, so she found an egg inside a cannon (4). It didn't contain a gift certificate for Have-a-Ball Sporting Goods (2), so it contained one for Captain Video Games. Jasmine won a gift certificate for Marina's Jewelry (3), so she found an egg in the birdfeeder (see above). By elimination, Regina won a gift certificate to Ristorante Via Venezia. She didn't find an egg under a trash can (5), so she found one in a fountain. By elimination, the egg found under a trash can contained the gift certificate to Have-a-Ball Sporting Goods. Keith didn't find this egg (5), so Paul did. By elimination, Keith found an egg under a picnic table.

Ellen	cannon	Captain Video Games
Jasmine	birdfeeder	Marina's Jewelry
Keith	picnic table	Dale's Music Shop
Paul	trash can	Have-a-Ball
Regina	fountain	Ristorante Via Venezia

20 HAZARDOUS HOBBIES

Margie took up birdwatching (4). A woman took up collecting model trains (1), so she's Beverly. Stuart didn't take up butterfly collecting (4), so Herman did. By elimination, Stuart took up juggling beanbags. He didn't used to do skydiving (4), bungee jumping or parasailing (6), so he used to do hang gliding. Herman used to do parasailing (2). Margie didn't used to skydive (4), so Beverly did. By elimination, Margie used to bungee jump. She dislocated her shoulder (3). Stuart didn't fracture his tibia (6) or displace a vertebra (5), so he broke his wrist. Beverly didn't displace a vertebra (1), so she fractured her tibia. By elimination, Herman displaced a vertebra.

Beverly	skydive	tibia	model trains
Herman	parasail	vertebra	butterflies
Margie	bungee	shoulder	birdwatching
Stuart	hang glide	wrist	juggling

21 ROYALTY CHECKS

Peter received seven checks in twelve months (intro), but received only two of these checks in consecutive months (5). This is only possible if he received checks in both January and December. If he had received a check for the book on Prince Rainier in February, then he would have received the remaining four checks in April, June, August, and October, which is impossible (4). Thus, he received a check for the book on Prince Rainier in November (1). He received four remaining checks in March, May, July, and September (5). He received a check for the book on Queen Beatrix in December (5). He received a check for the book on Margrethe II in September (6). He received a check for the book on King Harald V in July (4). He received a check for the book on King Juan Carlos in January (2). He received a check for the book on King Carl XVI Gustav in March (3). By elimination, he received a the book on Albert II in May.

January	King Juan Carlos
March	King Carl XVI Gustav
May	Albert II of Belgium
July	King Harald V
September	Margrethe II
November	Prince Rainier III
December	Queen Beatrix

22 AMY'S ADVICE

Amy's first response was to either Bewildered Boss or Perplexed Patron (1). Her response to Furious Father was "I would have gone ballistic" (2). Amy's advice to either Curious Cousin or Distraught Daughter was "Learn to speak Spanish" (4). Her second or third response was "You're only fooling yourself" (6). Amy's fifth response was either "Lighten up, dear" or "Not on your life" (7). This accounts for the five responses. Her first response wasn't "Lighten up, dear" (3), so this was her fifth response (see above). By elimination, her first response was "Not on your life." Her second response was to Bewildered Boss (5), so this was "You're only fooling yourself." Her first response was to Perplexed Patron (2). Her response to Curious Cousin wasn't "Lighten up, dear" (3), so it was "Learn to speak Spanish." By elimination, her fifth response was to Distraught Daughter. Her response to Curious Cousin wasn't fourth (4), so it was third. By elimination, her fourth response was to Furious Father.

1st	Patron	"Not on your life"
2nd	Boss	"You're only fooling yourself"
3rd	Cousin	"Learn to speak Spanish"
4th	Father	"I would have gone ballistic"
5th	Daughter	"Lighten up, dear"

23 SILENT FILM FESTIVAL

On Friday, the featured male star was either Buster Keaton or Douglas Fairbanks (4). Rudolph Valentino was featured on Saturday and Theda Bara on Tuesday (3). Clara Bow was featured on Monday and Fatty Arbuckle on Wednesday (6). Mary Astor and William Desmond Taylor were both featured on Thursday (1). Louise Brooks was featured on Friday and Mary Pickford on Saturday (5). By elimination, Betty Blythe was featured on Wednesday. Buster Keaton was featured on Tuesday (2). Douglas Fairbanks was featured on Friday (see above). By elimination, Charlie Chaplin was featured on Monday.

Mon.	Clara Bow	Charlie Chaplin
Tue.	Theda Bara	Buster Keaton
Wed.	Betty Blythe	Fatty Arbuckle
Thu.	Mary Astor	William D. Taylor
Fri.	Louise Brooks	Douglas Fairbanks
Sat.	Mary Pickford	Rudolph Valentino

24 GREEN ACRES, THE MUSICAL

Since Oliver sings "Just Us Two" (1), he can't be Mr. Kimball (2) and therefore he can't be singing either "Civil Service Blues" or "Down on the Farm" solo. Oliver's solo (5) isn't "Just Us Two" (2), "Civil Service Blues" or "Down on the Farm" (3), or "Hotcakes in Hooterville" (7), so it's "One Tiny Seed." The song that includes all five characters (1) obviously includes Mr. Kimball, so this is either "Civil Service Blues" or "Down on the Farm" (3). It also obviously includes both Lisa and Mr. Haney, so their only other song together is "Hotcakes in Hooterville" (7). Oliver, Lisa, and one other person sing "Just Us Two" (2). The other person isn't Mr. Haney (7) or Mr. Kimball (3), so he's Eb. He doesn't also sing "Civil Service Blues" (6), so this song doesn't include all five characters; therefore, "Down on the Farm" does. "Civil Service Blues" doesn't include Eb (6) and also doesn't include both Lisa and Mr. Haney (7), so it includes fewer than four characters; therefore, "Hotcakes in Hooterville" does. It doesn't include Mr. Kimball (3), so it includes Oliver, Lisa, Eb, and Mr. Haney. Eb sings exactly three songs (see above), so Lisa sings a different number (4), so she sings "Civil Service Blues." So does Mr. Kimball (3), but nobody else (1).

"One Tiny Seed": Oliver
"Civil Service Blues": Lisa and Mr. Kimball
"Just Us Two": Oliver, Lisa, and Eb
"Hotcakes in Hooterville": Oliver, Lisa, Eb, and Mr. Haney
"Down on the Farm": Oliver, Lisa, Eb, Mr. Haney, and Mr. Kimball

25 HANGOVER CURES

The five friends are: Jenny, the people who recommended Aleve and Excedrin, and the people who recommended jelly beans and olives (5). The person who recommended ginger snaps also recommended either aspirin or Tylenol (3), so she's Jenny. She didn't recommend jelly beans or Ritz Crackers (see above), so she recommended aspirin (1). The person who recommended cherries didn't recommend Excedrin (2), so he or she recommended Aleve. By elimination, the person who recommended Excedrin recommended Ritz Crackers. This person isn't Barbara or Calvin (1), or Larry (2), so she's Therese. Neither Barbara nor Calvin recommended jelly beans (1), so Larry did. A woman recommended ibuprofen (4), so she's Barbara, so she also recommended olives. By elimination, Calvin recommended Aleve and Larry recommended Tylenol.

Barbara	ibuprofen	olives
Calvin	Aleve	cherries
Jenny	aspirin	ginger snaps
Larry	Tylenol	jelly beans
Therese	Excedrin	Ritz Crackers

26 SCRABBLE BINGOS

One person's first name, last name, and bingo all have the same initial (4). This initial isn't B (1), P (2) or T (3), so it is A. Thus, this is Adrienne Ackerman and she placed the word "alchemy." Her bingo wasn't first (1), second (2), or third (3), so it was fourth. Neither Tami nor Torricelli placed the third bingo (3), so by elimination they placed the first and second bingos, in some order. Neither of them placed "tremors" (4), so this was the third bingo. "Beckoned" wasn't the first bingo (1), so it was the second. By elimination, "painting" was the first bingo. Prudence didn't place this word (4), nor did she place "beckoned," which was the the second bingo (2), so Prudence placed "tremors." Benny didn't place "beckoned" (4), so Tami did. By elimination, Benny placed "painting." Thus, he isn't Brown or Pantella (4), so he's Torricelli. Prudence isn't Pantella (4), so she's Brown. By elimination, Tami is Pantella.

First	Benny Torricelli	"painting"
Second	Tami Pantella	"beckoned"
Third	Prudence Brown	"tremors"
Fourth	Adrienne Ackerman	"alchemy"

27 UNCONVENTIONAL CONVENTIONERS

The person dressed as a Romulan likes *Voyager* best (1). The person who likes a series for its characters was dressed as either a Klingon or a Vulcan (5). The person who was dressed as a Ferengi likes either *Star Trek* or *Deep Space Nine* best (8). One person likes *Enterprise* for its special effects (9). This accounts for four of the five people. Sue isn't any of these (4), so she's the fifth. Either Anton or Marie was dressed as a Borg (2), so this person's favorite series is *Enterprise*. Jaime's favorite series is *The Next Generation* (6), so he likes it for its characters. He didn't dress as a Klingon (6), so he dressed as a Vulcan. By elimination, Sue dressed as a Klingon. Her favorite series isn't *Deep Space Nine* (3), so it's *Star Trek*. By elimination, the person dressed as a Ferengi likes *Deep Space Nine*. Neither this person nor Sue prefers a series for its acting (3), so the person dressed as a Romulan likes *Voyager* for its acting. Neither this person nor the person who like *Deep Space Nine* best is Marie (3), so Marie likes *Enterprise*. Anton likes a series for its overall storyline (7), so he likes *Deep Space Nine*. By elimination, Trey likes *Voyager* and Sue likes *Star Trek* for the episode plots.

Anton	Ferengi	*DS9*	overall storyline
Jaime	Vulcan	*TNG*	characters
Marie	Borg	*Enterprise*	special effects
Sue	Klingon	*Star Trek*	episode plots
Trey	Romulan	*Voyager*	acting

28 RIDING THE MUNI

Kyle's girlfriend is Monica (3). Noah took the L (5), so his girlfriend isn't Linda (intro). Linda's boyfriend also isn't Leroy (intro). She lives in West Portal (4), so her boyfriend isn't Jason (6), so he's Micah. He visited Linda in West Portal (see above), but didn't take the M or the L (intro), so he took the K (1). Jason went to Balboa Park (6), but didn't take the J (intro), so he took the M (2). Katy also lives in Balboa Park (7). Her boyfriend isn't Jason, who took the M (7). He also isn't Noah, because he took the L (5), which doesn't go to Balboa Park (2). Thus, Katy's boyfriend is Leroy. She lives in Balboa Park (see above), so Leroy didn't take the N (2), so he took the J. By elimination, Kyle took the N. Noah's girlfriend isn't Nona (intro), so she's Joanie. By elimination, Jason's girlfriend is Nona.

Jason	Nona	M
Kyle	Monica	N
Leroy	Katy	J
Micah	Linda	K
Noah	Joanie	L